HEROES AND WARRIORS

BOADICEA

WARRIOR QUEEN OF THE CELTS

JOHN MATTHEWS
Plates by JAMES FIELD

D0730801

Firebird Books

For the Caldecotts
For no other reason than its time they had one

First published in the UK 1988 by Firebird Books

Copyright © 1988 Firebird Books Ltd, P.O. Box 327, Poole, Dorset BH15 2RG
Text Copyright © 1988 John Matthews

Distributed in the United States by
Sterling Publishing Co, Inc,
2 Park Avenue, New York, NY 10016

Distributed in Australia by
Capricorn Link (Australia) Pty Ltd
PO Box 665, Lane Cove, NSW 2066

British Library Cataloguing in Publication Data

Matthews, John, *1948–*
    Boadicea : warrior queen of the Celts.——
    (Heroes and warriors series).
    1. Boudicca, *Queen, consort of Prasutagus, King of the Iceni*
    I. Title II. Series
    936.2′04′0924   DA145.3.B6

ISBN 1 85314 002 3

Series editor Stuart Booth
Designed by Kathryn S.A. Booth
Typeset by Colset Private Limited, Singapore
Colour separations by Kingfisher Facsimile
Colour printed by Butler and Tanner, Frome and London
Printed in Great Britain by Richard Clay Ltd, Chichester, Sussex

BOADICEA

WARRIOR QUEEN OF THE CELTS

In adopting the more traditional, but possibly now unfashionable, spelling of Boadicea for the great Celtic Queen's name, perhaps one should recall the preference of that noted British archaeologist Sir Mortimer Wheeler. He stated clearly that 'Boadicea' sounded like the sort of lady one would dine with, but never with someone called 'Boudicca'!

ROMAN BRITAIN

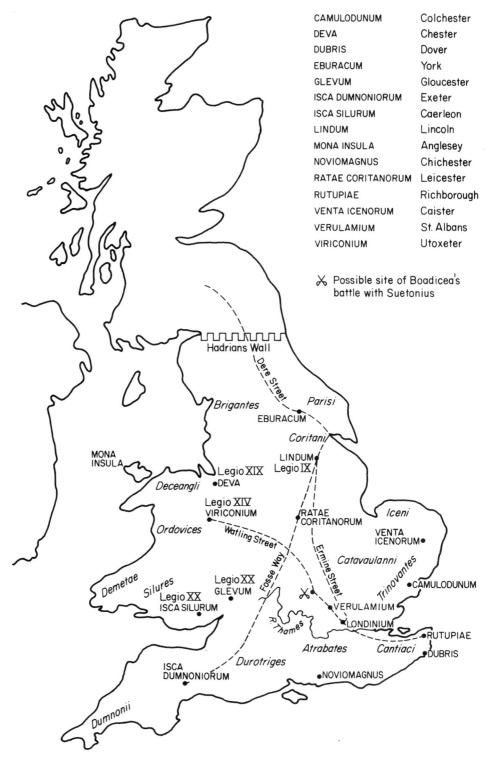

CAMULODUNUM	Colchester
DEVA	Chester
DUBRIS	Dover
EBURACUM	York
GLEVUM	Gloucester
ISCA DUMNONIORUM	Exeter
ISCA SILURUM	Caerleon
LINDUM	Lincoln
MONA INSULA	Anglesey
NOVIOMAGNUS	Chichester
RATAE CORITANORUM	Leicester
RUTUPIAE	Richborough
VENTA ICENORUM	Caister
VERULAMIUM	St. Albans
VIRICONIUM	Utoxeter

✂ Possible site of Boadicea's battle with Suetonius

Hadrians Wall

Dere Street

Brigantes

Parisi

EBURACUM

Coritani

MONA INSULA

LINDUM
Legio IX

Legio XIX
DEVA

Deceangli

Legio XIV
VIRICONIUM

RATAE CORITANORUM

Iceni

VENTA ICENORUM

Ordovices

Watling Street

Catavaulanni

Demetae

Silures

Legio XX
GLEVUM

Fosse Way

Ermine Street

Trinovantes

CAMULODUNUM

Legio XX
ISCA SILURUM

VERULAMIUM

R.Thames

LONDINIUM

RUTUPIAE

Atrabates

Cantiaci

DUBRIS

Durotriges

ISCA DUMNONIORUM

NOVIOMAGNUS

Dumnonii

With words that courage show'd, and with a voice as hie
(In her right hand her Launce, and in her left her Shield,
As both the Battells stood prepared in the Field)
Incouraging her men: which resolute, as strong,
Upon the Roman's rusht: and shee, the rest among,
Wades in that doubtfull warre . . .

Drayton: *The Polyolbion*

The British Celts

In 50 A.D. Ostorius Scapula, the Roman governor of the province of Brittannia, declared confidently that with the capture and transportation to Rome of Caractacus, already termed 'the last of the Celts', Celtic opposition to the Roman occupation would soon cease. Ten years later, he was proved drastically wrong when a violent revolt exploded in the territory of the Iceni, one of the largest tribes in Britain. Led by their Queen, Boadicea, they swiftly overwhelmed and massacred the populations of Camulodunum (Colchester) and Verulamium (St Albans), decimated a large part of the IX Legion, and went on to capture and burn London. Before she was finally defeated by the XX and XIV Legions under the command of Suetonius Paulinus, the name of Boadicea had become synonymous with terror and savage attack. She has ever since kept her place in the forefront of a small band of British heroes whose names have become part of a national heritage.

Yet who was this woman, who achieved such remarkable feats of war? What kind of warriors did she lead into battle with such resounding success? The story is a complex one and there are few reliable sources. Yet, a coherent picture does emerge if first we look at the kind of people from which she sprang.

The Celts
Our earliest impressions of the Celts come from classical sources. Posidonius, Strabo and Polybius described the Celts as tall, fair and ruddy-complexioned, loving the arts of war, feasting and drinking, famous hunters and fighters. To the Greeks, and later to the Romans, they seemed savage and barbaric: headhunters who tattooed themselves with strange patterns and went naked into battle. Yet their culture was far from backward. They loved literature and the arts, decorating everything – pots, mirrors, drinking vessels, weapons and horse-harnesses – with intricate and beautiful designs. Their sense of justice was almost as pronounced as their pride, which was considerable, and they were amongst the first people in Europe to develop a sophisticated system of laws to govern daily living.

Their religion, under the guidance of a druidic priesthood, was complex and highly mystical. They were close to the earth and its natural forces to a

5

The famous Gundestrup cauldron from Denmark shows Celtic warriors with long shields and spears, mounted men, and trumpeters – the latter must have added to the frightening noise produced by the warriors themselves.

degree unusual even for an ancient people. Their pantheon of gods was every bit as developed as those of Rome or Greece.

Diodorus Siculus, writing in the first century B.C. describes them as:

Terrifying in appearence, with deep-sounding very harsh voices. In conversation they use few words and speak in riddles, for the most part hinting at things and leaving a great deal to be understood. They frequently exaggerate with the aim of extolling themselves and diminishing the status of others. They are boasters and threateners and given to bombastic self-dramatization, and yet they are quick of mind and with good natural ability for learning.

While all of this is undoubtedly true as far as it goes, it is also something of a generalization. The classical writers tended to gloss over certain details, lumping *all* Celts together as one nation, irrespective of tribal differences. However, Tacitus did go so far as to distinguish racial types within the various areas of Britain. Thus the Caledonians were described as large and red-haired; the Silures or Welsh as shorter and with black curly hair, and the inhabitants of the South as resembling the Gauls.

This is an important distinction, which one has to keep in mind when discussing the Celts. The term 'Celtic' is itself really a linguistic or archaeological term for a people of very mixed origin. They seem to have come from an area in what is now the Steppelands of Russia, and to have migrated north and west in search of better lands and a warmer climate. Somewhere about 400 B.C., they settled in areas of Europe which today correspond to parts of Italy, Switzerland, Germany and Eastern France. They spoke a language which is the ancestor of contemporary Irish, Welsh, Gaelic and Breton, but they were so loosely confederated that to call them 'a people'

6

is really something of a misnomer. It would be more accurate to see them as a large number of fiercely independent tribes, who settled wherever they could find land suitable for farming and grazing their herds of cattle.

Though they were called *Keloi* or *Galatai* by the Greeks, and *Celtae* or *Galatae* by the Romans, we do not know for certain what they called themselves. *Cymru* 'the companions', is one possibility, which may also be translated more simply as 'the People'.

Tribal Society

The Celtic tribe, or *Tuath*, consisted of a number of families which according to Welsh and Irish laws extended back four generations. But, while a family was legally defined as man and wife (or wives, the Celts were polygamous) and their children, this could be further extended to include descendants of a common grandparent on the male or the female side.

The basic family unit was known as the *gelfine*, the larger as the *derbfine*, and within these two groups there was a shared responsibility for the apportioning of land and goods.

Wealth was calculated in terms of cattle and slaves. If a nobleman had a large herd of cattle, he hired out beasts to clients in return for a fee, and most important, for service. This meant that if a man owned a large herd, he also had more clients; the more clients he had the larger was the force of men he could put in the field in time of war, or to raid neighbouring tribes for more cattle, thus enabling him to raise more clients, and so on . . .

Caesar makes much of this in his description of the Celtic peoples, stressing a clear dividing-line between nobility and client. In reality, this was probably less distinct that it appeared to be. In a warrior society like that of the Celts, there were many opportunities for people to raise themselves to the status of the nobility, and with so much interrelatedness there was always a family tie of some kind to call upon.

To be a client did not imply curtailment of freedom. Class was defined according to whether or not one was free or unfree. The unfree, or slaves, consisted of men and women taken in raids, or of conquered people from earlier native races. The client gave service to a nobleman in return for cattle or goods: it was not uncommon for a chieftain to give a gold arm ring or torque to a warrior who had served him particularly well. Indeed, freedom was so very particularly important to the Celts, that it was doubly hard for them to accept Roman rule. After all, such rule meant disarming and paying fines for any insurrection, as well as involving a substantial loss of lands, which were given piecemeal to retired Roman army veterans. When the time came for Boadicea to raise her clan, as well as those of her neighbours, her first cry was one of 'freedom!'. It made her task far easier, even without the already powerful circumstances of her own treatment at the hands of corrupt Roman officials.

The overall ruler of the tribe, the patriarchal or matriarchal head of the most senior family, was known as a King, or *Ri*. There were thus many kings

This bronze figurine found near Rome gives a splendid idea of the warrior Celt as he appeared in battle – naked except for helm, belt and neck torque, he is poised in the act of throwing a spear.

and queens in the Britain of Boadicea's time, a fact which made it extremely difficult to form any kind of united front against the Romans; each petty ruler was fiercely independent of the others. Getting them to fight side-by-side was like trying to get two neighbouring dogs to fight for a single piece of territory.

The main tribes in Boadicea's time were – in the south of Britain – the Coritani, the Dobunni, the Catavellauni, the Atrabates, the Belgae, the Durotriges, the Trinovantes and her own Iceni. Their territory was probably bounded by the Wash on the east coast, and the Devil's Dyke, and what are now the towns of Stowmarket and Peterborough, taking in most of the fenland between. Since there were no such things as boundary markers – or if there were they are long-since vanished – it is virtually impossible to tell where the lands of one tribe and another met or divided. Nevertheless, reference to the map will give a general idea of the positions of the various tribes.

Warfare

We shall have good reason to look again at the way in which Boadicea fought her rapacious rebellion, but it is worth making a few preliminary remarks about the Celtic way of war, and to consider the (perhaps inevitable) reason why it repeatedly foundered against the disciplined wall of the Roman Legions.

8

The Celts were probably among the finest natural warriors in the world at that time, but they certainly knew nothing of discipline. Every warrior fought for himself, for his personal glory (which tended to be further exaggerated afterwards) and for booty – which comprised heads as much as weapons or jewelry. Again and again, we see the truth of Caesar's remark that only the first charge of a Celtic force was of any note – after that it was easy for the legionaries to mop up the remains! Yet, that first charge was certainly something to be feared. Here is Polybius' description:

> . . . the noise of the Celtic host terrified the Romans; for there were countless trumpeters and horn blowers and since the whole army was shouting its war cries at the same time there was such a confused sound that the noise seemed to come not only from the trumpeters and the soldiers but also from the countryside which was joining in the echo. No less terrifying were the appearance and gestures of the naked warriors in front, all of whom were in the prime of life and of excellent physique.

(trans: Ritchie)

The nakedness was in part caused by sheer bravado; in part a lack of sufficient body armour except among the rich and noble. Celtic blacksmiths were skilled workers, but never seem to have considered mass-producing armour or weapons for the ordinary warriors, who had to depend on the magical protection of the patterns painted on their bodies.

This certainly made them of striking appearance, with their limed hair combed into fantastic spikes or ruffs. Strabo tells us that it was socially

The head and mouth of a bronze Celtic trumpet found in Scotland. Accounts of Celtic warfare abound with descriptions of their war trumpets and the terror they inspired in their enemies.

9

unacceptable for a warrior to put on more than a certain amount of weight, and that there was a belt-tax levied whenever expansion went beyond a certain hole on the belt!

But by far the most feared and practical weapon ever used by the Celts must be the chariot. These light, two-wheeled carts, pulled by two strong and agile horses, had a single driver, and a warrior mounted behind him with a clutch of deadly throwing spears. Together they made a fighting team which was the scourge of the Roman legions.

But we must rid ourselves of one striking error which still lingers in the minds of many people even today. This is that Boadicea thundered onto the battlefield in a chariot with scythes on the wheels. No single example of such an equipped chariot has ever been unearthed in Britain, nor does Caesar mention them, despite having a good deal to say on the subject of chariots in general. Finally, as has often been wryly pointed out, a scythed chariot would have been as likely to inflict damage upon Boadicea's own warriors as on the Romans.

This being said, there is little doubt of the effectiveness of these vehicles in war. The Celts had certainly developed special skills when it came to fighting from a chariot – typically, perhaps, considering the nature of the Celtic personality, there was an element of bravado and sport about the whole thing. Thus, the warrior would often run out along the central pole, between the galloping horses, fling his spears at the enemy and then retreat to the bucking and careering platform in order to use it as base from which to fight with sword and mace.

Apart from mobility, which enabled the warriors to attack and retire at speed, the sheer noise of the chariot wheels thundering over the ground, mixed with the screams of the horses and the shouted war cries, must have been a shocking and terrifying sight.

Caesar certainly seems to have thought so, since he devoted several pages to the skills of the Celtic charioteers in his description of the fighting Britons. But just what they were pitting themselves against we must now examine.

The Roman Invaders

Julius Caesar had probably been receiving secret reports about Britain for some time before he made his first visit in 55 B.C. Certainly, he seems to have had a very good idea of what to expect when he arrived there. His account of the country is included in his history of the *Conquest of Gaul*, and is detailed and reasonably accurate. When it comes to describing the island he had this to say:

The island is triangular with one side facing Gaul. One corner of this side, on the coast of [now] Kent, is the landing place for nearly all the ships from Gaul, and points east; the lower

Bronze decorations from an Icenian chariot horse harness show the heights which the artistic abilities of the tribes could attain.

This reconstructed chariot is based on fragments discovered in a bog at Anglesey (Mona). It is of the kind that both the defenders of the island against Suetonius Paulinus and Boadicea's own warriors would probably have used.

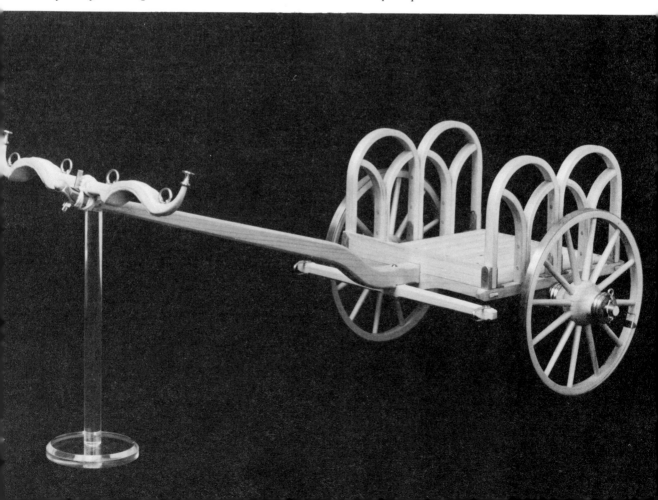

corner points south. The length of this side is about 475 miles. Another side faces west, towards Spain. In this direction is Ireland which is supposed to be half the size of Britain, and lies at the same distance from it as Gaul. Mid-way across is the Isle of Man, and it is believed that there are also a number of smaller islands, in which according to some writers there is a month of perpetual darkness at the summer solstice. Our inquiries on this subject were always fruitless, but we found by accurate measurements with a water-clock that the nights are shorter than on the continent. This side of Britain, according to the natives' estimate is 665 miles long. The third side faces north; no land land lies opposite it, but its eastern corner points roughly in the direction of Germany. Its length is estimated at 760 miles. And thus the whole island is 1,900 miles in circumference.

(trans: S. A. Handford)

It seems probable that this detailed, if rather baroque, description of the island, which Caesar had not seen and which indeed he never saw in anything like its entirety, is drawn in part from reports and from the works of earlier writers. The point being that, although this first attempt at invasion (as well as the one that followed it in 54 B.C.) were failures, Britain was very firmly established in Roman consciousness as a rich, fertile and ill-defended land which should clearly be a part of the Empire. It meant that however many years might elapse between, the Romans were bound to return.

And return they did, almost 100 years later, led by a very different commander – the remarkable Emperor Claudius. His campaign was staggeringly effective, and within two years Britain had become another province of Rome, with a large army of occupation installed in a growing network of forts strung out across the country.

Yet between the two invasion attempts, the one successful and the other not, links between Britain and Rome remained. On his second visit Caesar had negotiated a treaty which included an annual tribute and hostages. This

This aureus (sovereign) was issued around 51–2 A.D. to celebrate the Emperor Claudius' victory over the Britons and shows a triumphal arch bearing the word DEBRITTAN.

soon ceased after Caesar's assassination in 44 B.C. and with all the upheavals and civil wars that followed, it was some time before Rome again turned towards Britain with thoughts of conquest. Links of another kind, those of trading and political alliance, continued to be built up, thus affording Claudius, when the time came, both additional information for his campaign and a firmer foothold among the natives.

Claudius arrived in 43 A.D. – or rather his general Allus Plautius, whom he had commanded to go ahead and win every battle except the last – to which Claudius himself was to be summoned to take command – arrived with II, IX, XIV and XX Legions (some 24,000 men). They landed on a tiny island off the larger mass of Thanet, in what is now the south eastern county of Kent.

At first, they met with little resistance beyond the odd raiding party as they marched through the dark forest of the Kentish weald. But at the River Medway, they met a fully fledged war-band under the leadership of two brothers, Togodumnus and Caractacus, sons of the redoubtable King Cunobelinus (whom Shakespeare later made famous as Cymbeline). Cunobelinus had reigned over the powerful Catavellauni tribe as well as several tributary tribes for a number of years, and had left a strong and well-established kingdom to his sons' rule.

A long and ferocious battle took place at the mouth of the Medway estuary. But once the Romans had succeeded in crossing the stretch of water, victory followed. Against the splendidly carefree tactics of the Britons, the Romans were hard, ruthless and subject to an iron discipline which made them virtually undefeatable in battle. Again and again we hear of battle-maddened Celts hurling themselves against the Roman shield-wall, only to be repulsed. In contrast, the iron-shod boots of the legionaries pressed ever forward, step by step, until their adversaries were either exhausted or overwhelmed.

This gilded bronze eagle, discovered during the excavation of the Roman basilica at Silchester, may be part of a military standard. The eagles were carried into battle before each Legion and were regarded almost as gods. To lose such a standard brought disgrace and ill-luck to the legion it represented.

13

A model of the magnificent temple at Colchester dedicated to the Claudius, as it must have looked at the time of the revolt. It was never completed, and Boadicea destroyed it utterly when the defenders of Colchester took refuge there.

At London – then only a small trading post – a second battle ensued, in which Togodumnus fell and the Britains were routed. Plautius pushed on towards Camulodunum (Colchester), the Catavellauni capital, where he expected to stage a final victory.

Plautius sent word to Claudius in Gaul, and the Emperor – with reserve troops, elephants, and a sweating baggage train – proceeded there with full speed. Caractacus, desperate by now, and unable to raise any support from neighbouring tribes, fell back before the advancing Roman army and finally fled to Wales, where he could count on the help of wild Silures.

After this, British defence virtually collapsed; several chieftains, among them Prasutagus, Boadicea's husband, made haste to capitulate, and became tributaries of the invader in the hope of better terms of settlement. They became official allies of Rome with the status of vassal, and were allowed to continue nominal rule over their lands and people. Indeed, Cogidumnus of the Regnenses, became so romanized that an inscription found at Chichester in Sussex reads:

To Neptune and Minerva this temple is dedicated for the welfare of the divine house by the authority of Tiberius Claudius Cogidumnus king and legate of Augustus in Britain. . . .

14

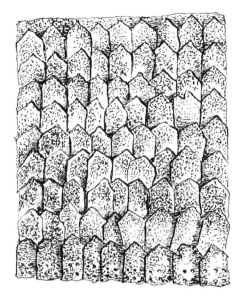

Though Britain could by no means be described as conquered, it was forthwith declared a province. Camulodunum, former capital of the Catavellauni, became the official centre of government, with Allus Plautius as governor and a procurator under him to handle tax-collection and civil affairs.

Work began at once on the building of a great temple to the gods of Britain and Rome, and after the death of Claudius in 54 A.D., it was dedicated to him as *Divus Claudius*, awarded, as were most emperors of the time, the status of godhead.

Fragment of Roman scale armour from Northumberland. Only officers or the more heavily armoured cavalry units would have possessed this kind of protection.

Britannia

This was far from the end of the story. In the ensuing four years, Plautius established bases at Ratae (Leicester) and on the borders of Wales. He sent his most able commander Vespasian (later to become Emperor himself) in command of the II Legion to subdue the Belgae and the Durotriges, who occupied regions roughly equivalent to the modern counties of Somerset and Dorset.

Vespasian fought thirteen battles against the natives including a massive assault against Maiden Castle in Dorset, where subsequent archaeological evidence suggests a massacre of men, women and children.

By the time Allus Plautius departed, handing over the governorship to Ostorius Scapula, all of Britain south of a line drawn across from Bath to London and including most of Essex had been subdued. The IX Legion was established at Colonia (Lincoln), the II at Isca (Caerleon) and the XIV and XX as Viroconium (Wroxeter).

The capture of Caractacus took another two years and was only accomplished by the treachery of Queen Cartimandua of the Brigantes, who handed him over together with his family into Roman hands. He was taken to Rome

15

itself, where he so impressed Claudius that he was awarded a pension and allowed to live out his life there. He is said to have looked at the buildings of the eternal city and remarked: 'And yet the owners of these must needs covet our poor huts?'

It was shortly after this that Ostorius Scapula made his confident statement about the end of British resistance, which was to be proved so dramatically wrong. However, something like a *Pax Romana* did exist in Britain for a time, and the new province began to experience some of the more welcome effects of Roman rule. The countryside became more settled, and the steady flow of trade goods, pottery, wine and cloth, began to enter the country. The pro-Roman dignatories were encouraged to adopt the ways of their conquerors, building houses for themselves in the style of Roman villas, complete with hypercaust (underfloor heating) and vineyards.

Though the tendancy thus begun was not to reach fruition for 100 years after the initial period of conquest, it began almost as soon as the last active resistance ended – or was thought to have ended – with the capture of Caractacus.

There was also a move to bring in settlers, mostly legionary veterans who were granted allotments of land in return for which they were expected to keep an eye on the native population in case of any signs of revolt. The first of these was established in the old British capital of Camulodunum, and thus became one of Boadicea's first targets when she began her revolt against the conquerors. Ostorius' hope seems to have been that while the regular legions were away policing less-settled areas, the presence of the veterans at Camulodunum would keep things stable in the south – another error for which the Romans were to pay dearly.

Thus stood matters at the beginning of 59 A.D. when Suetonius Paulinus arrived to become the new military governor of Britain.

Power of the Druids

It has been stated by more that one commentator on Roman Britain that the Druids had a great deal to do with the forging and fuelling of the revolt – partly because of their natural animosity towards the invaders, but mostly in retaliation for the destruction of the great Druid college on Anglesey.

This may be partly true, but the situation was considerably more complex than it would at first appear. Much of this complexity stems from previous misconceptions about the nature of druidism and the activities of the Druids in Celtic Britain.

Indeed, so much has been written about the Druids that is *total* fiction that it is now extremely hard to extract the truth. Yet they were certainly a power

Before the battle which ended the Icenian revolt, Boadicea harangued her troops from the step of her chariot. Flourishing a spear, she demanded vengence for the wrong done to her.

in Britain (as in Gaul) and the classical accounts we do possess tell us a certain amount.

The Druids did not, as is still commonly believed, build Stonehenge, or indeed any of the great megalithic monuments with which Britain is so liberally littered. Indeed, though they may have used these sites on certain occasions, they seem generally to have worshipped (or at any rate gathered) in groves of sacred trees. The idea that these were primarily oak trees may stem from the connection made by Greek lexicographers between their word for oak, *drus* and the Celtic (Irish) word *druïd*.

The Origin of the Druids

We do not know the origin of the Druids, though it is possible that they migrated to Gaul and later Britain from the area of the Mediterranean or North Africa, sometime during the Bronze Age.

This has lead in turn to speculation as to whether they were influenced by the teachings of Pythagoras (around 500 B.C.) which spread from classical Greece into Alexandria and thence to the rest of the Western world. They seem to have shared a belief in reincarnation, the transmigration of souls and the sacredness of all life, animal as well as human. There are also tantalizing references to a Greek traveller named Aristeas of Proconnesus, who visited Britain (or a country which may have been Britain) and found there a place where men worshipped Hyperborean Apollo in a circular stone temple in the midst of a plain. Stonehenge? Possibly. But were these the Druids? They do indeed seem to have worshipped the sun – or at least to have taken care to observe its risings and settings. But there is no specifically solar deity in the Celtic religion – despite a number of solar heroes whose strength increased and decreased with the rising and setting of the sun.

Diogenes Laertius (200–250 A.D. records a meeting between Alexander the Great and a wandering Celt, who may or may not have been a Druid. It has been pointed out by at least one commentator that when asked if he feared anything, his reply: 'Not so long as the sky never falls or the sea does not burst its bounds' does have a familiar ring to it. The same formula is repeated several times throughout Celtic literature, almost as a kind of invocation, though whether it was of Druid origin we cannot say.

Shamanism

Another Greek, Pliny the Elder, in a dissertation on the medicinal properties of mistletoe, gives us the famous connection of this plant with the Druids, who were said to hold it in the highest esteem: so much so that any tree on which it grew – it is a parasite – was at once regarded as sacred.

The reasons for this may well lead us to a very important factor in our understanding of druidism. One of the properties of mistletoe not mentioned by Pliny is the hallucinogenic drink which is distilled from it. The method by which this was attained is long since lost – mistletoe is deadly poison in its natural state – but it may have given the Druids their means of entry to the

Before her triumphal compaign, Boadicea sought the guidance of Andraste, the goddess of victory in Celtic Britain. Boadicea released a hare from beneath her cloak; according to which path it ran, so was victory or defeat determined.

The labels in the diagram, from top to bottom, are:

cobbles of 3rd period road
clay
clay — clay
remetalling or 2nd period road
cobbles and gravel
sand
quarry stones
hard gravel
quarry stones
yellow sand or chippings
clay

0   20 ft

Typical construction of a Roman road. The system of roads built by the Romans enabled messages to be delivered speedily and troops to be moved more effectively. This lonely stretch crosses Wheedale Moor in Yorkshire.

18

inner realms of the spirit where they could learn remarkable truths and make prophecies for the future of the people.

This puts them on a par with the shamans of other ancient people, who were the preservers of tradition and the inspirers of the tribes in their care as well as guarding their religious truths and knowledge. This seems precisely the function of the Druids in Britain and Gaul.

A bronze boar, possibly from a Celtic war-helm. It was recognised as a symbol of strength, fierceness and potency. Helmets and chariots bore decorations in the shape of the boar to give their wearers added strength and protection. The clan totem of the Iceni was either a horse or a boar.

Druids and Druidism

Even assuming this to be true, there is still a basic confusion between the Druids themselves and druidism. It would probably be a mistake to view this as in any way the 'official religion' of Britain, either during Boadicea's reign or at any other time. The druidic colleges, like the one despoiled by Suetonius Paulinus on Anglesey, was one of several such establishments both in Britain and Ireland. But the Druids who ran these were historians, archivists, lawgivers and teachers rather than priests in the properly understood meaning of the word.

If we see them in this light, much of the speculation and fantasy concerning the Druids fall away. They taught the arts of poetry and song, compiled genealogies and generally preserved the history of the people. Much of this they kept in their heads, expecting their pupils to learn immense amounts of poetry and lore by heart. They were also lawgivers, as Caesar's testimony shows:

They act as judges in practically all disputes whether between tribes or between individuals; when any crime is committed, or a murder takes place or a dispute arises about an inheritance or about a boundary, it is they who adjudicate the matter and appoint the compensation to be paid and received by the parties concerned.

These three Celtic shields from different periods and places show the consistency of design over the years. Made from wood or leather, and covered with decorations in bronze, they protected the warrior from shoulder to knees.

All this seems a very far cry from the usual image invoked by the word 'Druid'; that of blood-soaked rituals performed at dawn over stone altars, or for that matter the traditional cloaked, white-bearded patriarch who seems to belong rather in a Biblical scene than in a picture of ancient Celtic life.

In retrospect it seems probable that the blood sacrifices talked of frequently by commentators, though they may indeed have taken place, were presided over by a native priesthood which had little or nothing to do with the Druids. Certainly the Celts were a war-like, often savage people (as indeed were the Romans, despite their much-vaunted civilization) but they were no more or less so than any other ancient tribal society. The picture sometimes presented of Druid sacrifices with men held in wicker cages which were then set on fire, is almost certainly far from the truth.

What we should try to see is a body of enlightened men and women, to which membership was a highly sought honour, who endeavoured to preserve and educate, and who above all sought to hold in trust the sacred heritage of the people.

Thus, we have on the one hand the 'Druids-as-known', and on the other 'Druids-as-wished-for' – the former being of a very different tenor from the latter.

Rebellion

Teachers then, guardians of wisdom and tradition, poets, historians and genealogists; these were the primary functions of the Druids, all of them important within the Celtic world. This would indeed have given them

20

considerable power and influence, and had they chosen to give support to Boadicea it would have been more than sufficient to tip the scales in her favour. That they did indeed give her this support seems likely. Equally likely is the effect that news of Suetonius Paulinus' attack upon Anglesey would have had. Tacitus gives a vivid portrait of the event – though it should be noted that he does not designate the Druids as targets.

On the beach stood the adverse array, a serried mass of arms and men, with women slipping between the ranks in the style of furies in robes of deathly black and with disheveled hair they brandished their torches; while a circle of druids, lifting their hands to heaven and showering imprecations, struck the troops with such an awe at the extraordinary spectacle that, as though their limbs were paralyzed, they exposed their bodies to wounds without an attempt at movement. Then, reassured by their general, and inciting each other neer to flinch before a band of females and fanatics they charged behind the standards, cut down all who met them, and enveloped the enemy in his own flames.

(trans: John Jackson)

Queen of the Iceni

For many years she was called Bunduica and believed to have a co-regnant named Voadicia. Then, for a while, she became Bonducca and later still the familiar Boudica or Boadicea. Whatever, her real name means 'victory', the early spellings resulting from poor mediaeval manuscript transcription and inaccurate Elizabethan versions of Tacitus, whose account of her story was unknown at all until the sixteenth century.

We can follow the mutations of her name far more easily than we can put flesh onto the bones of her life. We know much about the military details of the revolt of 61 A.D.; we know her end; and we know something of what drove her to begin. Yet, though her name is widely known, we really know very little more.

How old she was when she died we can infer only from the fact that she had two teenage daughters (thus making her between thirty and forty); we know from Dio Cassius what she looked like:

In stature she was very tall, in appearance most terrifying, in the glance of her eye most fierce, and her voice was harsh; a great mass of the tawniest hair fell to her hips; around her neck was a large golden necklace; and she wore a tunic of divers colours over which a thick mantle was fastened with a brooch. This was her invariable attire.

(trans: E. Cary)

Beyond this there is little to add. Imagination suggests a strong and stubborn woman married to a weak husband. Prasutagus' haste to bend the knee to Roman rule must have gone hard with his wife, who was almost certainly of equally royal blood, but had no love for the conquerers. Even if she had not at first felt animosity, her later treatment at the hands of greedy and unscrupulous officials would only have increased her dislike to full hatred.

21

The Celtic warrior and his
charioteer. In pitched battle they
were an unbeatable team – fast,
manoeuvrable and deadly.
Drawn by two swift and sturdy
ponies, they would hurl themselves against the opposing force
and discharge their spears. Then
the warrior would leap down and
engage the enemy directly, while
the charioteer withdrew to the
fringes of the battle.

We can speculate that she received warrior training which fitted her for the
battles to come. The Celts made no distinction between men and women
when it came to fighting, and many ran training schools for teaching warriors of both sexes. Certainly, the Romans had a healthy regard for them as
adversaries, as the historian Ammianus Marcellinus tells us:

A whole troop . . . would not be able to withstand a single Gaul if he called his wife to his
assistance. Swelling her neck, gnashing her teeth and brandishing her sallow arms of
enormous size, she begins to strike blows mingled with kicks as if they were so many missiles
sent from the string of a catapult.

The Iceni

Of the tribe which came to be at the middle of the revolt, we know only that
it appears to have been made up of two distinct groups of people, whose
arrival in Britain dates from between 500 B.C. and 150 B.C. The first influx
probably came from the area of Europe now occupied by the Netherlands and
Belgium, the second from the Marne Valley area in France. The first were a
peaceable people, who mixed with the earlier native population and taught
them the skills of iron smelting. The second were of a more militant, warrior
class who were better armed and accoutred than their forbears, and soon
overran large tracts of what are now Lincolnshire and Essex, setting up places
from which they ruled over the former inhabitants as a military elite.

In time, these elements blurred into a more homogenous whole which is
recognizable in the Iceni as they appear at the time of Prasutagus and Boadicea.

Judging by treasure and quantities of coins discovered in the areas known
to have been occupied by them, the Iceni seem to have been a wealthy tribe.
This fact must have contributed both to Prasutagus' desire not to lose out to
the Romans, and the strong desire of the latter to acquire as much as they
could.

There seems to have been a well established Icenian coinage from as early as
10 B.C. and this has given us a clue to their probable totem animal – the
tribal guardian who protected them from ill-luck, monsters or attack. This is
a curious beast which at once bears a strong resemblance to a boar and a horse.
Depending upon which period one examines, this seems to alter from genera-

22

tion to generation, almost as though the coiners themselves were unsure – though doubtless this was a matter of style rather than uncertainty.

There are no coins from the period of Prasutagus' reign, a fact which has led some commentators to believe that client-kings were not allowed to mint their own coinage once the Romans had established theirs. Perhaps Prasutagus was simply being cautious and trying to retain a hold over his considerable wealth in order to provide for an always uncertain future. On his death, he was found to have willed half his kingdom to the Emperor – an undoubted contributory factor in the causes of the revolt.

The Horse Breeders

The Iceni seem to have possessed another kind of wealth – horses. There are persistent rumours of their being horse breeders, though on the face of it this would seem unlikely due to the large areas of marshland in the Iceni country of eastern Britain.

Boadicea's army certainly contained a significant number of chariots. These required a special kind of horse; small, compact, powerful and agile.

The romantic image of Boadicea and her daughters as portrayed in this nineteenth century group which stands in the Civic Hall, Cardiff.

In fact, the kind of horse which archaeological evidence has found most frequently in Britain. They may have been a cross breed of the cold-blooded beasts found in much of Northern Europe, and the Arab 'barb'.

There is really no firm evidence to point to the Iceni as the possessors of large herds of horses, but we are allowed to speculate. Perhaps the shrewd Prasutagus chose this means of conserving his wealth, while at the same time providing the chariot beasts necessary for sudden or unexpected warfare. So, to this kingdom, suddenly in 60 A.D., Boadicea ascended as queen; Prasutagus' death had sown the seeds of the rebellion soon to follow.

In the Runs of the Iceni

We have little or no evidence of the Icenian situation prior to and after the death of Prasutagus. All that we can do is surmise and draw parallels from the prevailing Celtic society which was shortly to fragment in Britain.

At the death of Prasutagus, Britain had been nominally subdued to the Roman yoke some eighteen years. The idea was still new enough and repugnant enough for tribes to think of revolt, but there is no evidence that Prasutagus personally desired this. With the steady encroachment of the Romans upon tribal territory, from the south-west northwards, any local king would have realised the inevitability of having either to totally defeat the Roman army, or of coming to terms with the fact of Imperial control. By becoming a client king, sworn to be federate to Rome, Prasutagus wisely took the most reasonable alternative. Tribes to the south of him had already realised the impossibility of military superiority; other tribal kings had discovered cultural and political benefits from peaceful secession and alliance.

Such a decision would not have pleased the more traditional of his followers who, inculcated with generations of ancestral pride in their battle prowess and respect for the royal bloodlines of their race, would have urged a fight to the death. Older men, perhaps retired war veterans themselves, would have urged younger relatives to vaunt their prowess and make ready for war. They would have roused their blood with daring deeds of past glory – rival tribes being raided, women carried off, insults avenged. This was contrary to Prasutagus' policy.

We have no knowledge of Prasutagus' age at his death. He is unlikely to have been a young or middle-aged man. The description of Boadicea suggests a mature woman, and it was usual for a woman to be up to one or two generations younger than her husband in an age where women frequently died in childbirth. Prasutagus was probably an elderly man or at least one who had the best part of his active life behind him. The city of Camulodunum was at the borders of his territory, steadily developing in testimony of Rome's conquering magnificence. Knowing himself to be near the end of his life and wanting to ensure the future existence of his tribe, he acceded to the rationalist's way out: he swore allegiance. How he restrained his hot-headed tribesmen – all of whom would have voiced their very strong objection to his decision in open council – is not known. But restrain them he did, keeping himself and his tribe within the *Pax Romana*.

The Honour of the Tribe

This peaceful solution was dear bought. Icenian honour was brought low. Whatever obvious resistance and opposition might have been voiced was countered by the sheer order and organisation of Roman conquest. This insidious web of bureaucracy soon wound its way into every aspect of Icenian life. Taxes had to be paid and where Icenian families would doubtless have groaned at tribute owed to their overlord in any case, giving tribute to Rome via him was a worse case. Roman officials would have been attached to Prasutagus' court as subtle reminders of conquest and their different standards of elegance and behaviour would have been resented.

What struck at the heart of Icenian honour was the reading of Prasutagus' will, leaving half his kingdom to the Emperor. While this document was obviously drawn up in secret, and probably under a good deal of political duress (Prasutagus doubtless had Roman officials who dropped hints on the correct form in such matters), the shock to Boadicea must have been considerable.

We only know that Boadicea was governing in the name of her daughters, who were Prasutagus' legal heirs under British law, though not the only likely or possible ones under Celtic custom. It is possible that the girls were as yet unmarried and that suitable husbands had to be found for them from within the prescribed royal branches of the family: men who were mature and able enough to rule in the name of their wives and carry on the good name of the Iceni in battle. It is on this point of the viability of female heirs that the subsequent outrages should be balanced. Roman law did not make allowance for such inheritance of mere females; British law made no distinction.

As Boadicea was herself mature and able, she assumed the throne in their name and thus held the tribe together. There is no thought of her being a cipher in tribal policy. She may have sternly and privately disagreed with her husband's policies, while supporting him publicly in his seemingly cautious regime of submission to Rome. Her subsequent behaviour leads one to believe that she was his chief wife; used to issuing orders, to being obeyed and capable of laying down the law to her husband. Her anger at his betrayal of their life's work must have been extreme. But, while she later gave rein to her anger, there is no suspicion that she was uncontrolled or unprincipled. Her duty was clear: to bind the tribe to her and to protect her daughters' rights.

It was Rome's mistake that its commanders did not take Boadicea seriously – either as a royal woman or as a mother. Female rulers were risible to them. They had the standing joke of Cleopatra in Egypt, with whom Julius, that erstwhile conqueror of Britain, had a brief dalliance. Queens were for seducing, for manipulating. Rome should have been warned: queens were also treacherous, dextrous in attack and ruthless when cornered. Cleopatra took poison to avoid the inevitable Roman triumph in which she would have been dragged when Augustus Caesar finally caught up with her.

No one thought of seducing Boadicea or marrying her off to another pliant client king: she was a woman of maturity, her character was indissolubly formed, her years of political sexuality behind her. She was not a commodity. But her daughters were.

These unnamed girls were probably in their early teens. They were a dangerous factor in the political balance. To the Roman mind, virgin daughters of a dead king might be as hazardous as a massed army of Icenian tribesmen – let only one man of power marry one of them and power could be focused and the flame of revolt be fanned.

The Treacherous Lioness

When the officials finally came to strip Boadicea of her governing rights, they clumsily drew all the wrong conclusions. The Icenian queen's righteous anger could be cooled by the scourge. The daughters could be conveniently deflowered and made less desirable to a nobleman of discernment. It was customary for the public executioner to deflower virgins before their deaths, lest the gods be offended, within Roman tradition. The young daughters of attainted consuls were inevitably raped before being thrown to their deaths or strangled.

That Boadicea might have bided quietly at home after such treatment was not to be countenanced. While she might not care on her own behalf, she had her daughters to fight for. Rome had raped the sovereignty of Britain; now it had raped the daughters of an Icenian king, women of the royal kingmaking blood. The Romans would have done better to kill all three women. A directionless battle might have ensued: one easily won by Rome. As it was, the Iceni rose on the command of an outraged mother. The 'treacherous lioness' as the chronicler Gildas called her, was aptly named by him. 'The lion may look proud and disdainful in his tree, but it is the lioness who hunts and brings home prey for her cubs'. The Icenian queen was now ready to rend any who harmed her offspring.

The Face of Revolt

It is never easy to judge the exact measure of cause and effect, especially long after the events in question. In the case of the British revolt of 61 A.D., there are two clear contributory factors, but far more that lay beneath the surface. The temporary *Pax Romana* was only superficial; beneath it the native population seethed with unrest and anger. In many cases, their lands had been taken

away from them, with little or no recompense, and (as at Camulodunum) given out in parcel form to retired Roman army veterans. Added to this was the very nature of the petty Roman officials placed over them for the task of collecting taxes and tributes and seeing that everything conformed to Roman neatness. In effect, it was the behaviour of some of these officials which touched off the smouldering fuse which was to ignite the south under Boadicea's leadership. Given the nature of Prasutagus' will, the government officials moved in to collect the extraordinary tribute to the Emperor. Finding only Boadicea and her daughters to oppose them, they went about their business as crudely as possible – in the hope, we may assume, of getting all.

At least, this is how things seem to have been. The current Procurator, Catus Decianius, seems to have been a greedy man, not above taking a large share of any goods that were to hand – as were his officers, mostly retired army men and slaves.

Thus, given the treatment she received and the seemingly pre-planned rape of her daughters, small wonder at Boadicea's rage. She and her family had been outraged in every way possible and her tribe made to suffer. She herself, as Queen of the Iceni, had been publicly humiliated.

This Roman helmet of the Imperial–Gallic type from a reconstruction by H. Russell-Robinson dates from roughly the period of the Icenian rebellion and is the kind that would have been worn by the Legionaries. It is made of iron and would have borne a crest.

27

BRIGANTIAE

A Romanized relief of the Celtic goddess Brigantia, here identified with Roman Minerva, whose attributes she bears – her spear and wings of victory. The Icenian goddess, Andraste, of whom no representation remains, may have been similar.

Goddess of War

Before the revolt was even properly under way, Dio Cassius puts into the mouth of Boadicea a noble speech worthy of the greatest Roman orators, with metaphors ransacked from classical literature in which she compares herself favourably with Nitocris, Semiramis and Messalina. It is here that we read of her invocation to the Icenian goddess Andraste, to whom she speaks as a woman to a woman.

The goddess Andraste is only mentioned in Dio Cassius: we have no other information about her attributes or mythos. It seems reasonable, since Celtic scholars give the meaning of Andraste as 'Invincible', that she was a goddess

28

of battle. She may well have been akin to Brigantia, the titulary goddess of the Brigantian tribes of northern Britain.

Dio Cassius tells how Boadicea let a hare out of a fold of her garments and set it speeding towards the oncoming enemy as a means of divining the battle's outcome. Whichever side it ran on was considered the auspicious side. The hare has ever been a beast of the shapeshifter, a creature of the moon. The nature of Boadicea's invocation to Andraste leaves us in no doubt what she is said to have thought of the Romans. She impunes their soft comforts, their pederasty and their womanish emperors (particularly Nero). She takes to herself the attributes of the goddess and invokes her protection upon her tribe: 'Mistress, be thou alone our leader!'

It is possible that the wholesale slaughter of civilians which followed was in the nature of a ritual sacrifice to propitiate Andraste in her sacred groves. Certainly, Andraste's hare ran before the chariots of the Iceni for a good many months before her protection expired.

Paulinus and the Druids

Meanwhile, Suetonius Paulinus as military governor, a hard and dedicated soldier with experience of fighting natives in Spain and Gaul, and a knowledge of mountain terrain which may have influenced his choice, began an action which was to antagonize further the already angry Britons.

He had already spent the first two years of his office, from his arrival in 59 A.D. to the spring of 61 A.D., familiarizing himself with the particular problems facing him in Britain. It was clearly not a 'settled' province, and at the end of this time he was convinced that the main backbone of native resistance centred on the Druids, and in particular their college on Mona (Anglesey).

He was probably only partially correct in this belief; but apart from any Druid involvement, Mona had certainly become a sanctuary for a considerable number of refugees and dissidents, who remained there awaiting an opportunity to stir up trouble against their oppressors.

At least, this is how Suetonius Paulinus saw matters, and thus, in the spring of 61 A.D., not long before Catus Decianius sent his collection squad into Iceni territory, Suetonius marched on Anglesey with every intention of laying it waste.

It seems safe to assume that the Roman general had already secured large areas of the territory occupied by the Silures and the Deceangli, and that he had wintered at Deva (Chester) on the River Dee. From there, he had overseen the building of large numbers of flat-bottomed boats with which to cross the Menai Strait. As Tacitus' laconic narrative tells us:

By this method the infantry crossed; the cavalry, who followed, did so by fording or, in deeper water, by swimming at the side of their horses.

Yet even as Suetonius' army celebrated its victory by cutting down the sacred

trees on the island, news came that the Queen of the Iceni had risen in revolt and that the Trinovantes had joined with her. The south was in flames.

This bust of the Emperor Claudius was found in the river Alde, where it may have been dropped by Boadicea's army after the destruction of Colchester. Perhaps it stood in the entrance to the great Claudian temple where the defenders made their last stand.

The Fall of Camulodunum

Suetonius immediately sent orders to Cerealis Petillius, the commander of the IX Legion, to quell the rebellion. However, it took this general precious time to gather a large enough force from the scattered forts and camps in which they were billeted. In that time, Boadicea marched on the city of Camulodunum (Colchester) and totally destroyed it.

Had Cerealis moved more quickly, or had the Procurator Catus Decianius been able to send more than the meagre 200 ill-armed veterans he managed to scrape together in response to a panic-stricken call from the citizens of

30

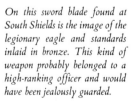

On this sword blade found at South Shields is the image of the legionary eagle and standards inlaid in bronze. This kind of weapon probably belonged to a high-ranking officer and would have been jealously guarded.

31

Camulodunum, things might have been very different. As it was, the Britons met with virtually no resistance until they reached the temple of Claudius, hated symbol of their subjugation and a permanent reminder of the man who had conquered them.

In fact, the temple, which had been dedicated to Claudius shortly before his death in 54 A.D., was still incomplete. However, its massive walls were the only defensible area in the city, since the walls of the earlier Roman fort had been pulled down to make room for the expanding township.

Here, then, the desperate defenders, men, women and children, gathered to make their last stand, hoping to hold out long enough for relief to arrive from the IXth Legion. They were not to know that Boadicea had laid a carefully prepared ambush in the woods along the road towards Camulodunum. There, her army cut the Legion to pieces, leaving only a handful of cavalry, with which Petillius ignominiously escaped.

Thus, no help was forthcoming, and effectively the citizens of Camulodunum were doomed. The Iceni and the Trinovantes, who had been forced to contribute to the cost of building the Claudian temple, destroyed it utterly, along with the entire population, estimated at some 2,000 people, including army veterans and pro-Roman Britons living in the town.

Suetonius Strikes

Two things then happened. The Britons, elated to a point of madness by their success, began rampaging across the country, looting and burning any settlement of Roman or pro-Roman standing they could find. Suetonius Paulinus, with news of the fall of Camulodunum ringing in his ears, took a fast galley to Deva and pushed on at full speed with a detachment of cavalry towards Londinium (London) which lay directly in the path of Boadicea's victorious army.

Fortunately for the governor, the Celts were still celebrating their success and had scattered across the country, otherwise they might have been waiting for him as they had for Petillius outside Camulodunum – when events would probably have been very different. As it was, the Governor of Britain arrived to find the people of Londinium in a state of petrified fear. The Procurator, Catus Decianius, whose actions had helped fuel the rebellion, had fled to Gaul from where he disappears in recorded history.

The only hope for London was in Suetonius Paulinus. Having grasped the gravity of the situation, he realized that his only hope lay in abandoning London to its fate, in the hope that it would hold up Boadicea long enough for him to gather sufficient troops to face her on ground of his own choosing.

Therefore, he did the only thing possible in the circumstances – offered his protection to any refugees who wished to accompany him on the road south. There he could billet them on the still pro-Roman king Cogidumnus, who seems to have willingly promised his support. (He must have had to make a swift decision on which side to back: had Boadicea triumphed he would

Camulodunum (Colchester) was the centre of Roman government in Britain. It was here that Boadicea first struck, overwhelming the city and reducing it to rubble and ashes.

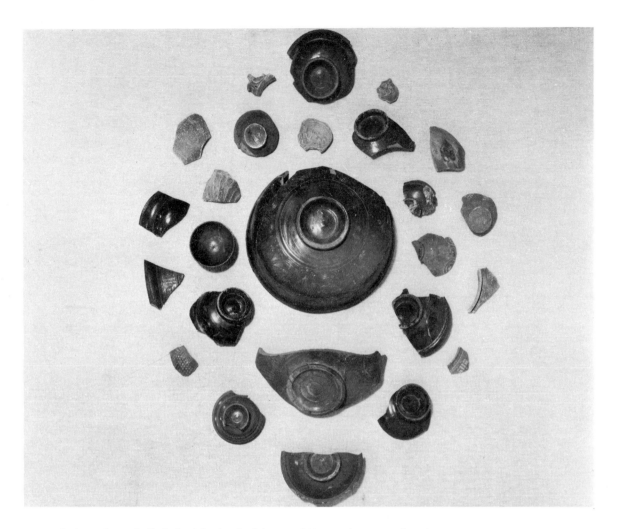

certainly have been killed; had he backed her and Rome become the victor, his comfortable career would have been swiftly over.)

A number of citizens elected to travel with Suetonius and straggled south. It was now early July of 61 A.D. Nothing stood between Boadicea and the huddle of houses and official buildings shambling beside the River Thames.

A selection of pottery from the period of the rebellion. They are blackened and burned from the holocaust which struck the city in 65 A.D.

The Sack of London

Dig anywhere within the compass of the earliest Roman settlement in London and at a certain level – about twenty feet down – you are bound to encounter a layer of ash and blackened pottery-shards. This is the legacy of Boadicea's sack of Londinium. She left it a smoking ruin scarcely days after Suetonius had withdrawn.

In those days, London extended barely two miles from its centre – the crossing-place of the River Thames at (now) London Bridge, where two roads

The Roman army, led by Suetonius Paulinus, met the Iceni at Mancetter, near Watling Street, and defeated them utterly. Boadicea took a fatal dose of poison after the battle, rather than suffer the ignominy of capture.

met which lead north-east to Camulodunum and north-west to Veralamium (St Albans) and Silchester.

Londinium had been founded by the Romans around 43 A.D. on two hills either side of the Walbrook stream where it issued into the Thames on its northern bank. Shortly afterwards they erected a bridge across the river at more or less the same point of the present day London Bridge, and began making roads to connect with the Channel port of Rutupiae (Richborough). This at once made Londinium an important supply depot for incoming ships supplying the armies in the North, South and West. However, its importance at this juncture was subsidiary to that of Camulodunum, which had become, to all intents and purposes, the centre of Roman government in the South of the country. After the revolt, when both sites had been levelled, emphasis shifted from Camulodunum to Londinium, which rapidly became the most important commercial and administrative centre in Britain. A new governor's palace was erected, which rivalled all previous structures, and soon bath houses and a magnificent basilica followed.

In Boadicea's time, however, none of this existed; only a scatter of tumbledown houses, some villas owned by rich merchants, a temple and a few shops and warehouses. Yet despite its size, London was undoubtedly busy and crowded with merchants, traders and the inevitable population which nearly always grows up around such commercial and mercantile centres.

Lewis Spence, in his book on the rebellion, describes the probable appearance of Londinium at this time as follows:

> . . . on the whole, with the exception of a few shrines and executive buildings the 'architecture' of the Londinium of this phase . . . seems mostly to have been composed of timber plastered over and dwellings of Romano-Celtic type, mainly constructed from that wattle-and-daub material of the Britons . . . The general aspect must have been that of a somewhat irregular and impermanent-looking straggle of comparatively small buildings, villas, booths, shacks and hutments falling riverwards down the slope from the present site of Leadenhall to the mouth of the Walbrook . . .

Moreover, there seem to have been no defences at all – archaeological investigation has revealed no evidence of any walls – even of timber – until after the rebellion. Neither was there any military presence, so that it must have seemed to Boadicea that she was about to harvest a fruit over-ripe for the picking.

Why did the majority of the citizens of Londinium – an estimated 20,000 – remain behind when Suetonius offered them his protection? Firstly, it is by no means easy to pack up all one's goods and follow the swift pace of a Roman cavalry unit whose commander is anxious to make good time. Secondly, there were a great many women and children in the township, who were unable to travel far or fast. Thirdly, many simply refused to believe their danger.

Rumour of the sack of Camulodunum had certainly reached them, but there were many who believed that Boadicea would come no further south, or that she would bypass Londinium and attack Verulamium instead. One

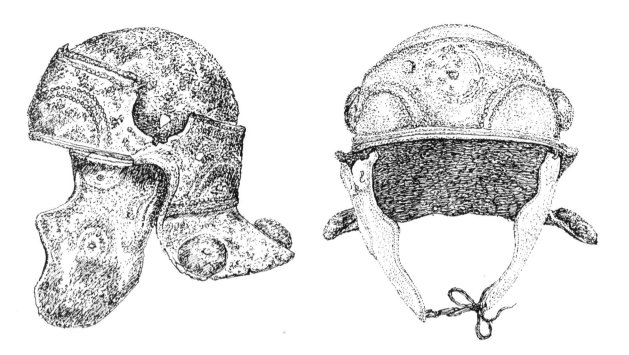

suspects that many did not believe in the seriousness of the situation, even after Suetonius had made his brief, dramatic appearance and withdrawal. The rest simply accepted the end as inevitable, and while a few made hasty preparations to defend the township, others simply waited.

Two views of a Roman helmet of the Auxiliary cavalry type, dating from the period of the rebellion: the left side with its distinctive cheek-piece; and the front view of a reconstruction by H. Russell-Robinson.

The End of Londinium

The defenders almost certainly never knew what hit them. Boadicea's host now numbered around 20,000 and they simply overwhelmed the township, putting its community to the sword and burning all the buildings to the ground. Doubtless the citizens gave their lives dearly, but they had no chance against the battle-crazed Britons, being ill-armed and ill-prepared for the devastation that was to come.

Dio Cassius' account of what happened is precise, though it makes grim reading:

Those who were taken captive by the Britons were subjected to every form of outrage. The worst and most bestial atrocity committed by their captors was the following. They hung up naked the noblest and most distinguished women and then cut off their breasts and sewed them to their mouths, in order to make the victims appear to be eating them; afterwards they impaled the women on sharp skewers run lengthwise through the entire body. All this they did to the accompaniment of sacrifices, banquets and wanton behaviour . . .

(trans: E. Cary)

Exaggeration? Perhaps; though atrocities of this kind were not unknown at the time, and the Britons had by this time been fuelled by hatred and success to a point where they were less a host than a deadly machine which destroyed everything in its path. Dio Cassius was a Roman and wrote some time after

35

the events, so there may well be an element of exaggeration. But Boadicea clearly felt no regrets. She led the sacrifices to the goddess Andraste, whose name appears to mean Victory, but who surprisingly enough appears nowhere else in the history of the Celts.

Boadicea must already have been planning the next stage in her campaign, for though she had little control over the warriors who wanted to spend time exacting a full recompense for past wrongs done to them, she knew that ahead lay Verulamium, and somewhere beyond it Suetonius Paulinus and the Legions. Time was against her and she may have chafed at the delay caused by the excesses of her tribesmen. She also knew the impossibility of trying to do more than direct them, in their own time, towards the next objective. It was this delay which cost her the rebellion and, untimately, her own life.

Suetonius and the Legions

What kind of man was it that Boadicea faced in her battle to free Britain from Roman domination? Giaus Suetonius Paulinus was a hardened soldier with several campaigns behind him. He had fought in North Africa against the Moors some years previously, leading an army as far as the Atlas Mountains in his urge to quell an incipient rebellion. It was probably at this time that he attained consular rank, though he had to wait a further seventeen years before being given the military governorship of Britain.

He arrived to find the province in a state of some confusion. The previous governor, Quintus Verianius, had lived less than a year before succumbing to the climate. Though the south seemed peaceful, the northern tribes, especially the Brigantes, were a constant threat to Roman security in the island.

Verianius had been a milder man, though still an able soldier, whose brief had been to take a more conciliatory attitude to the native population. Suetonius set out to crush any revolt and to police the island with his Legions in such a way as to allow no opportunity for insurrection. His first major campaign, as we have seen, was against the Druid sanctuary on Anglesey, which was carried out with typical military precision and iron determination. Suetonius was, in short, a professional and typically Roman soldier.

The Legions in Britain
The Legions within Suetonius' command at this time were the II Augusta, IX Hispana, XIV Gemina and XX Valeria. The II was probably stationed at Isca (Caerleon) and in the Severn and Wye valleys; the IX at Lindum (Lincoln); while the XX was ranged along the borders of Brigantia. The XIV was first of all stationed at Viroconium (Wroxeter) but moved to Deva (Chester) at the start of the campaign against the Silures and the attack on Mona (Anglesey). It had, in all probability, been drafted from the Rhine

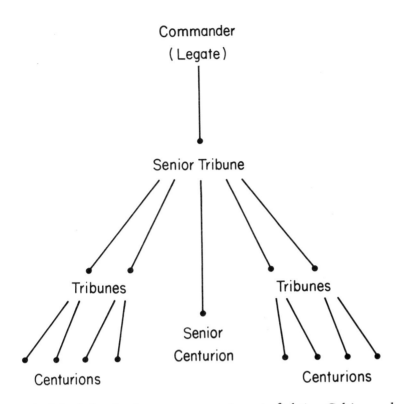

Commander
(Legate)

Senior Tribune

Tribunes

Tribunes

Senior
Centurion

Centurions

Centurions

army, which had already the greatest experience in fighting Celtic peoples in Gaul and Germania.

Staff structure within the Roman Legions.

In general, a legion consisted of 6,000 men. These were divided into ten cohorts, further divided into eight centuries. Nine of the cohorts were normal, with the tenth, 'double' century forming the elite core of the legion under the command of a senior centurion.

Initially, only those born into Roman citizenship were permitted to join the army, but this soon became impracticable and it became normal to confer citizenship along with a commission. Thereafter, the legions consisted of people from many nations, and one might find within any one legion Goths, Gauls, Scythians, Samartians or Asturians from Spain. In the same way, Celtic warriors from Britain were sent to fight on Rome's furthest frontiers.

Each legionary served a term of 20 years, during which time it was possible for him to rise through the ranks to the position of centurion, commanding eighty men and answering directly to a prefect or tribune. There were five of these tribunes, four of equal rank and a fifth who answered directly to a commander.

In addition, a number of prefects commanded several cohorts of auxiliaries, which normally consisted of native militia, fighting in native dress and with their own weapons, rather than the mailed uniform of the regular legionary. Unlike the legions, they were regarded as irregular troops, and though they served five years longer than the legionaries, they received lower pay and seem to have been given the hardest and most arduous tours of duty.

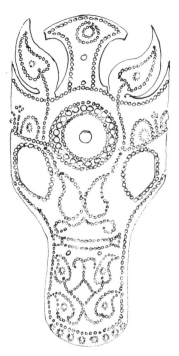

Any soldier could re-enlist at the end of an initial term of duty – but there was no discharge from the Legion except in exceptional circumstances, or because of severe wounds. Men who had lost limbs or were otherwise incapacitated were often kept on as camp servants, but there was no official pension until they had served for a number of years. Of course, it was the apportioning of native lands to retired veterans which caused such ill-feeling among the tribes at the time of the rebellion.

The regular soldiers were trained to a standard which stands comparison with modern day commando or special forces. They had to be able to scale embankments, leap ditches and swim rivers and straits – as well as marching for twenty miles in five hours carrying a full pack, which might contain three days' rations and a mess tin, together with a saw, axe and shovel. This last item, along with a wicker-work basket, was used to throw up an earthen bank around their camp at night. This was standard procedure whether the stopping time was one night or ten.

Of course, each man also had to carry his weapons and the armour he wore. This was usually of leather strengthened with strips of iron, though some senior officers wore mail shirts of overlapping scales.

Their weapons consisted of two, six-foot throwing spears, with hardened wooden shafts and iron heads. It was this *pilum* which was to inflict such terrible havoc among the close-packed Celtic warriors in the final battle of the rebellion. Additionally the legionary carried a short stabbing sword called a *spatha*, and a dagger. These were intended for close work, and the typical action of a Roman unit was to form a shield-wall behind which they advanced, step by inexorable step, striking between swiftly raised shields and then rapidly recovering themselves. Their long shields, made of several layers

38

Typical image of a Roman officer, so hated by the Celts. From the tomb of Marcus Favonius Facilis, Colchester.

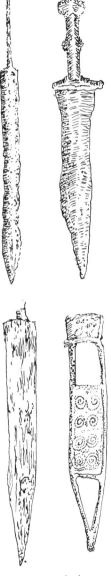

Weapons carried by every legionary included the spatha (two-edged sword), pugio (dagger) and gladius (broadbladed sword), here shown with a decorated scabbard.

of wood, were designed to protect the body from neck to thigh, and were thus ideal for such work.

Their only really weak spot was their legs and feet, which were virtually undefended in order to give them better mobility; there must have been many casualties with wounds in these areas. Otherwise they were virtually invulnerable, with their hard leather helmets protecting their heads and necks. Once a powerful wedge of legionaries moved forward against an enemy, there was little that could stop them short of a head-on cavalry charge.

Rome's own use of cavalry was still limited at this time – the usual tactic being for the mounted units to remain on the wings, while the infantry did the hardest part of the work. Then they would fling into the fray to mop up the remaining enemies or those who tried to flee.

Within the Legions were positions for masons, surveyors, engineers and sappers, as well as signallers, medical orderlies, armourers and clerks. Some of these specialized troops were present in every Legion, which had to be self-sufficient and self-governing during its long months away from base.

Once a foothold had been established in Britain by Allus Plautius in 43 A.D., immediate building was instituted to set up an expanding network of forts and armed camps throughout the country. These were connected by a system of roads which were still recognised as being one of the finest achievements of their day and whose remains as highways can still be seen.

Against such disciplined, well-armed and highly trained soldiers, moving at speed along a growing system of roads, the wild tribesmen had little chance when it came to direct conflict. On the one hand, Britons were experts at guerrilla tactics, as they demonstrated in their destruction of the XX Legion outside Verulamium. On the other hand, the Romans were past masters of the art of flexible movement in battle, with a complex system of signals which enabled a commander to move units of force at will.

A fast system of couriers with connecting post stations along the whole length of the roads enabled messages to be sent at great speed. Hence, the way that Suetonius was able to get word of the rebellion while he was still far away in Wales.

All of this made the Roman Legions probably the best army in the world. So Boadicea's initial success is all the more impressive – though she had elements of surprise on her side, as well as a feeling of moral indignation which acted as fuel to her already enraged followers. Let us look now at the final act in the drama, and at the meeting between these two implacable foes.

The End of the Revolt

Finally succeeding in gathering her battle-sated warriors around her, Boadicea now pressed on towards Verulamium (St Albans), the third important township on which she unleashed her fury. However, unlike both Camulodonum and Londinium, Verulamium was almost totally British, its population consisting almost entirely of Catavelaunii, a tribe so staunchly pro-Roman they had earned the hatred of their neighbours. There was probably also an element of tribal rivalry present in this, which the general atmosphere of slaughter and warfare restimulated.

Whatever the reasons, Verulamium met the same fate as the other towns. The fine Roman-style houses, the basilica and other public buildings were burned to the ground and the inhabitants wiped out with as much savagery as had been meted out to the Roman citizenry of the other townships.

Classical accounts of the revolt estimate the number of dead at 70,000. This is almost certainly an exaggeration, given substance by the passage of time; but enough evidence exists to suggest a truly frightful slaughter of men, women and children. It seemed that nothing could stop Boadicea from sweeping across the country and either killing or driving out every Roman in Britain. Only Suetonius Paulinus now stood between her and this objective, and he still lacked the forces to meet the Iceni and Trinovantes in direct conflict with any real hope of winning.

Therefore, he continued to withdraw, and according to Dio Cassius began to grow short of food – a reasonable supposition if his base was still in Wales and his supplies correspondingly far removed. By now, he had been joined by the rest of the XIV Legion, as well as detachments of the XX and II Legions, and daily awaited the arrival of the remainder of the II, who were then stationed at Isca Dumnonorium (Exeter) under the temporary command of Peonius Postumus, the camp prefect.

For some reason Poenius failed to answer the call to join the XIV and XX Legions – possibly because he was under attact from the Durotriges, who had also risen in revolt following Boadicea's dramatic victories.

When the conflict was finally over, this unfortunate officer fell on his sword rather than face the disgrace that would have resulted from his failure to follow a direct order – thus also incidentally robbing his own Legion of a share in the honour of defending the province against the terrible Iceni queen.

Reconstruction of a Roman villa of the kind which may well have been occupied by Codgidumnus, the staunchly pro-Roman King of the Atrabates. Many similiar unprotected farmsteads between Colchester, London and St Albans, fell victim to Boadicea's war-host.

The Last Battle

We really have no idea where the final confrontation between Boadicea and Suetonius took place. A site in what is now Leicestershire, near Mancetter, to the south-east of Atherstone and close to the line of Watling Street, has been suggested by Graham Webster, the leading authority on the revolt. Paulinus, he points out, would have chosen a position to give him the greatest tactical advantage, and going on the information included in Tacitus, he suggests that:

It was at the approach to a narrow defile which meant that the Britons were forced to advance into a front of diminishing width: the greater their force the more packed they would have become in their eagerness to reach the Romans

(*Boudica*: Webster)

Behind lay a thick forest, on rising ground that gave plenty of protection to

41

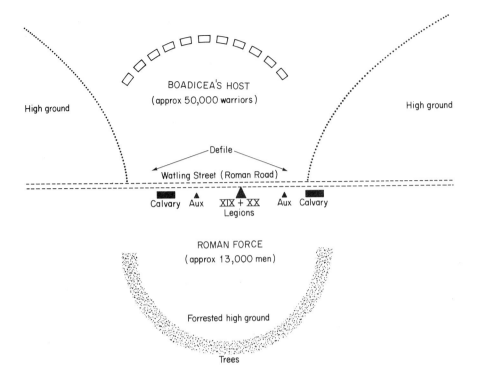

High ground

BOADICEA'S HOST
(approx 50,000 warriors)

High ground

Defile

Watling Street (Roman Road)

Calvary Aux XIX + XX Aux Calvary
Legions

ROMAN FORCE
(approx 13,000 men)

Forrested high ground

Trees

Likely plan of the battle between Boadicea and Suetonius.

Paulinus' rear. Ahead the ground was open, affording no cover to the advancing Britons. It seems quite astounding in retrospect that Boadicea allowed herself to be drawn into giving battle in such terrain; but by this time her army – which has been estimated at anything between 100,000 and 230,000 – had gained a frightening momentum. The Britons believed that nothing could stop them – after Camulodunum and the IX Legion, after Londinium and Verulamium, they would simply roll over the Roman army and leave nothing but dead in their wake. So certain were they of victory that they had even brought their wives and families with them in huge wagons. These now formed a semi-circle behind the war-host, effectively enclosing them between two walls – the Romans in front and their own people behind. Tacitus says that women and children were even seated on top of the wagons to view the spectacle of Rome's defeat.

Against this imposing host of Celtic warriors were ranged an estimated 11–13,000 Roman soldiers, consisting of the XIV Legion, detachments of the II and XX at the centre, as well as cavalry and auxiliaries on the wings.

Both Dio and Tacitus record the speeches of the respective leaders before the battle – Dio's is lengthy, bombastic and wholly unlike anything a British leader would have uttered. Tacitus, whom we must remember was reporting events actually witnessed by his uncle, may get closer to the truth. At least we get a feeling of the kind of words that might well have resounded above the shouting, screaming, chanting warriors of the British side, or over the silent, waiting ranks of the legionaries:

Mounted in a chariot with her daughters before her, she rode up to clan after clan and delivered her protest: it was customary, she knew, with Britons to fight under female captaincy, but she was avenging, not, as a queen of glorious ancestry, her ravished realm and power, but, as a woman of the people, her liberty lost, her body tortured by the lash, the tarnished honour of her daughters.

(trans: J. Jackson)

The gods themselves were on their side, she continued, as witnessed by their just success. One Legion they had destroyed already, the rest were skulking in their camps and would never face so vast an army as their own. Let the men go home if they wanted, the women would finish this on their own! We may imagine Boadicea's harsh voice ringing out across the field, her red hair flaming, her strong arms raised, shaking a bloodied spear towards the Roman army.

Even Suetonius, according to Tacitus, broke his customary silence, commanding his men to 'ignore the noise and threats of these savages', pointing out that there were more women than men in their ranks and that they would soon give way before soldiers who had beaten them so often in the past. To this few, he claimed, lay the honour of the Legions and of Rome, so:

Keep close order, when you have thrown your javelins, push forward with the bosses of your shields and swords, let the dead pile up, forget all about plunder, win the victory and it's all yours.

(trans: Webster)

And so the Britons came on. There was little room for the usual wave of chariots, the shouted insults, thrown spears and swift withdrawals; the whole mass of the British host advanced together, and were met with a hail of Roman javelins, unyieldingly followed by a second. Many fell, and then the Legions began their advance. Supported by cavalry on both flanks to prevent any of the Britons escaping, they pressed forward with the inevitability of a steel ram. Three wedges were driven deep into the press of Celts who had no room to swing their long swords against the short *pila* of the legionaries.

They were cut down in swathes and began to retreat, only to find their backs hampered by their own wagons and families. In a few hours, it was over. Hundreds, perhaps thousands of Britons lay dead in great mounds; women and children and old men, even the oxen which had pulled the carts to the site were slain and blocked all retreat. In all, some 40,000 Britons probably fell that day, against less than a quarter of that number of the Romans. We cannot know the exact figures, and Tacitus and Dio undoubtedly exaggerate.

Dio Cassius tells us that Boadicea fell sick and died, although whether in captivity or not, he does not state. Tacitus inclines to her taking poison. In whatever manner her death took place, the revolt was over.

If Boadicea did indeed take poison, the reasons are not far to seek. She had probably been captured and had no wish to be packed off to Rome to form the central tableau of the Conquest of the Britons in the triumphal train of Suetonius. Like Cleopatra of recent memory, she preferred the honourable

A gladius, the Roman legionary's favourite weapon. Crouched behind his huge shield, he flicked the blade in and out, thrusting rather than hacking. An excellent weapon for close work, the grip is made of bone or wood, and the leather scabbard shown here decorated with medallions of victory or the god of war.

43

way out. It is also possible that she had other reasons for no longer clinging to life. History does not tell us of the fate of her daughters. Had the Romans captured them in battle they would doubtless have told the world. The girls would have been either summarily executed or perhaps married to men of no account. It is likely that they perished in battle, possibly the last affray.

Without her daughters to fight for and bereft of the protection of Andraste – whose nemetons she had liberally watered with the blood of Romans – Boadicea died.

No other woman after her has left such a mark upon British history. In terms of leadership, determination and ruthlessness not even Eleanor of Aquitaine nor Margaret of Anjou (the queens of Henry II and Henry VI respectively), nor Elizabeth I, possessed Boadicea's stature. She remains alone, a solitary pyre on which the hopes of Britain's independence smouldered fitfully and were consumed utterly.

It is impressive testimony that both Tacitus and Dio Cassius treat Boadicea's impossible plight with sympathy, while decrying her bloodthirsty slaughter of their fellow citizens. Barbarian and female she might have been, but her cause was a just one. To a Roman, honour and courage were virtues which cancelled many faults. These qualities Boadicea had in plenty. Both historians accord her the tribute of a worthy and noble adversary. Dio said:

Let us, I say, do our duty while we still remember what freedom is, that we may leave it to our children not only its appellation but also its reality. For, if we utterly forget the happy state in which we were born and bred, what, pray, will they do, reared in bondage?

Aftermath

Reinforced by 2,000 legionaries from Germany, as well as 1,000 cavalry and 4,000 auxiliaries, Suetonius now set about a systematic and terrible retaliation against the tribes of southern Britain. Calling upon the name of *Mars Ulator*, god of vengeance, he marched through Iceni and Trinovant territory, burning crops and farmsteads and slaughtering any Britons he found. He seems, indeed, to have become somewhat deranged, pursuing his trail of vengeance with a savage determination, almost as though some of Boadicea's blood-lust had communicated itself to him after her death. At any rate, he kept the army 'under canvas' for the remainder of the year – which must have made him extremely unpopular with the legionaries, who would normally have wintered in the comparative comfort of a stone fort.

Only the appearance of a new Procurator, Julius Classicanus, put an end to these events. Some kind of quarrel seems to have occurred between the two men, and we may suppose that it was over Classicanus' desire to take a more moderate line with the Britons.

In dispatches to Rome, he requested the recall of Suetonius, and finally got his way in the following year. A new Governor, Petronius Turpitilianus, duly arrived, whose policy was one of mediation rather than attrition, and by the end of the year the province had begun to settle back to a more peaceful existence.

Boadicea's failure after her initial triumph, remained in the minds of the Britons sufficiently to deter them from making another serious attempt at revolt. The northern tribes were either forced into submission or contained behind Hadrian's Wall and Britain became in every way a Roman province, though the shockwaves sent out by Boadicea's unparalleled success and the violence and wholesale slaughter caused by the revolt, continued to cause ripples in Rome's attitude to her provinces for some time thereafter.

It may be said that the rebellion finally helped to make the state of things in Britain better than they had been before – there seems to have been a genuine attempt to recognize the tribes as civilized people rather than as painted savages. Temples were raised to Celtic gods in the guise of their Roman equivalents – though the Druids, their power broken by Suetonius, were never again permitted to re-establish anything like a formal organization.

Not until the gradual break-up of the Empire some 500 years later caused the withdrawal of the Legions, was there any effort on the part of the Britons to reassert themselves. By which time they had a new adversary to contend with – the Saxons. But by then many of the tribes had been thoroughly romanized, and the face of Britain had changed forever.

Boadicea Remembered

Boadicea is best remembered for her courage and leadership which was, however, no match for the iron discipline of the Legions. As Caractacus had learned before her, it was virtually impossible to weld the fiery, independent tribes into anything like an army. Once the momentum of their early victories was spent, they collapsed, and were cut down. Rome triumphed as she had always done, though suffering a blow which she would never quite forget.

Boadicea assumed her place in history as one of the truly great heroines of Britain and is remembered as a champion of the people – though she has had a chequered career at the hands of writers through the ages. The irascible sixth century historian Gildas called her 'a treacherous lioness'; while at the other extreme the poet Tennyson apostrophized her as a great English heroine.

She was, first and foremost, a warrior queen: proud and unbending to the Roman yoke. Justice was certainly on her side in the beginning, and she could scarcely have been expected to appeal to Rome for redress of the wrongs done to herself, her family and her people. She took the only way, and blazed a trail of blood which has never been forgotten. The revolt of 60 A.D. is only a minor episode in the history of Rome, as indeed it is of Britain. Yet, in the end, one has nothing but respect for Boadicea and her wild tribespeople. As Lewis Spence memorably, if rather extravagantly, put it:

Vaster than any form in the early saga of this sea-fortress of the north looms the shade of Boadicea, triumphant even in name and memory, among the world's greatest examplars of womanly vigour, a goddess in armour descending to the succour of a folk enslaved.

The Notitia Dignitatum

The *Notitia Dignitatum* is a list, compiled in the third or fourth century A.D. of the principal officers and their areas of responsibility within the Empire. It was transcribed and copied successively up until the seventeenth century, when it was probably destroyed, and much of it is thereby corrupt. Within a larger whole, the *Notitia Orientis*, and the *Notitia Occidentis*, which deal respectively with the eastern and western halves of the Empire, are set the chapters dealing with the province of Britannia. It gives a fascinating glimpse of the division of Britain into areas with forts and officers responsible for units of the legions. Although the *Notitia* dates from after the period of the rebellion, it is unlikely to have changed much in the preceding years. Also, this organization itself may have been a result of the revolt, after which things became much tighter within the province.

The text is that of O. Seeck (1876) incorporating the amendments of A. L. F. Rivet and Colin Smith (1979), with translations from the Latin original by Caitlín Matthews. The inclusion of? in place names indicates tentative identification.

Vicarius Britanniarum was the substitute for an absent or deceased provincial governor. He was responsible for the parts of Britain which, like the rest of the Roman Empire, was divided into provinces and dioceses for easier administration: *Maxima Caesariensis* was South East Britain; *Valentia* was north of the Wall; *Britannia Prima* was South-East Britain; *Britannia Secunda* was Britain north of the Humber; *Flavia Caesariensis* included the Midlands and Wales.

Comes litoris Saxonici per Britanniam Count of the Saxon Shore in Britain was directly responsible for the following officers and dispositions:

Praepositus numeri Fortensium, Othonae Military Officer of the Fortenses regiment at Bradwell

Praepositus militium Tungrecanorum, Dubris Military Officer of the Tungrecani regiment at Dover

Praepositus numero Turnacensium, Lemannis Military Officer of the Turnacensi regiment at Lympne

Praepositus equitum Salmatarum Branodunensium, Branoduno Military Officer of the Dalmatian cavalry, Brancaster

Praepositus equitum stablesianorum, Gariannonensium, Gariannonor Military Officer of the Stablesiani cavalry, Burgh Castle

Tribunus cohortis primai Baetasiorum, Regulbio Tribune of the First Baetasium Cohort, Reculver

Praefectus legionis secundae Augustae, Rutupis Prefect of the Second Augustinian Legion, Richborough

Praepositus numeri Abulcorum, Anderidos Military Officer of the Abulcorium regiment at Pevensey

Praepositus numeri exploratorum, Portum Adurni Military Officer of Scouting (Spying) regiment, Porchester.

The Dux Britanniarum Duke of Britain was responsible for the following officers:

Praefectus legionis sextae Prefect of the VI Legion at York

Praefectus equitum Dalmatarum, Praesidio Prefect of the Dalmatian cavalry at?

Praefectus equitorum Crispianorum, Dano Prefect of the Crispinian cavalry, Doncaster? Jarrow?

Praefectus equitum catafractariorum, Morbio Prefect of cataphracts?

Praepositus numeri barcariorum Tiridiensium, Arbeia Prefect of the Tiridatian regiment, South Shields

Praefectus numeri Nerviorum Dictensium, Dicti Prefect of Nervian regiment, at Wearmouth?

Praefectus numeri vigilum, Concangios Prefect of the Watch, Chester-le-Street

Praefectus numeri exploratorum, Lavatres Prefect of the Scouting regiment, Bowes

Praefectus numeri directorum, Verteris Prefect of the Pathfinding regiment, Brough

Praefectus numeri defenscrum, Braboniaco Prefect of the Defensive regiment, Kirkby Thornton

Praefectus numeri Solensium, Maglone Prefect of the Solensium troops, Old Carlisle

Praefectus numeri Pacensium, Magis Prefect of the Pacensian troops, Burrow Walls?

Praefectus numeri Longovicanorum, Longovicio Prefect of the Longovi troops, Lanchester

Praefectus numeri supervenientium Petrueriensium Derventione Prefect of the Superventores regiment, Malton

The Dux Britanniarum also had responsibility for 24 further Prefects and Tribunes posted along the Wall.

Chronology of the Rebellion

Much of Lewis Spence's information, on which the following is based, has been superceded by modern archaeological evidence. Nevertheless, there seems no reason to quarrel with his suggested time-scale of events.

60 A.D. Death of King Prasutagus.

61 A.D. **Early March** Suetonius departs for Anglesey.
The outrages on the Icenian royal family take place.
Mid March–May Partition of Icenian territory proceeds. Annexation to Roman colony.
Mid March–May Suetonius makes preparations to attack Anglesey.
May–June Hosting of the Iceni and other tribes.
June Suetonius attacks Anglesey and proceeds to demolish native monuments, etc.
End of June Suetonius receives news of unrest among the tribes.
Early July Boadicea attacks Camulodunum.

61 A.D. **Early July** Suetonius arrives at Londinium.
Londinium sacked.
Suetonius retreats across the Thames in the direction of Regnum, conveying the fugitives from Londinium part of the way to that place.
Mid July Verulamium sacked.
Mid July–Mid August Suetonius takes up a position south of the Thames.
Mid August He recrosses the Thames and marches northward to Londinium.
End of August Meets Boadicea in battle.
September–October Suetonius gathers forces in Britain into one army 'to finish the war' and ravages the territories of the hostile tribes.
October–November Reinforcements sent from Germany. They go into winter quarters.

Further Reading

Brannigan, K. *Roman Britain* Readers Digest, 1980.
Caesar *The Conquest of Gaul* (trans. S. A. Handford) Penguin, 1951.
Clayton, P. *A Companion To Roman Britain* Phaidon, 1980.
Cunliffe, B. *The Celtic World* Bodley Head, 1979.
Dio Cassio *Roman History* (trans. E. Cary) Loeb Classics, 1925.
Durant, G. M. *Britain: Rome's Most Northerly Province* Bell, 1969.
Frere, S. *Brittania* RKP, 1967.
Gildas *The Ruin of Britain* (trans. M. Winterbottom) Phillimore, 1978.
Goodall, D. M. & A. A. Dent. *The Foals of Epona* Galley Press, 1962.
Lindsay, J. *Our Celtic Heritage* Weidenfeld, 1962.
Mellett, M. *Warrior Queen* Pan Books, 1978.
Merrifield, R. *The Roman City of London* Longman, 1965.
Newark, T. *Celtic Warriors* Blandford Press, 1986.
Norton-Taylor, D. *The Celts* Time Life International, 1976.

Piggott, S. *The Druids* Thames & Hudson, 1968.
Ritchie, W. E. & J. N. G. *Celtic Warriors* Shire Press, 1985.
Rivet, A. L. F. & C. Smith. *The Place-Names of Roman Britain* Batsford, 1979.
Robinson, H. R., *The Armour of Imperial Rome* Arms & Armour Press, 1976.
Ross, A. *The Pagan Celts* Batsford, 1986.
Scullard, H. H. *Roman Britain, Outpost of Empire* Thames & Hudson, 1979.
Smurthwaite, D. *Ordnance Survey Complete Guide to the Battlefields of Britain* Webb & Bower, 1984.
Spence, L. *Boadicea* Hale, 1937.
Tacitus *The Agricol & the Germania* (trans. H. Mattingly) Penguin, 1944.
Tacitus *The Annals* Books XIII–XVI (trans. J. Jackson) Loeb Classics.
Webster, G. *Boudica: The British Revolt against Rome AD 60* Batsford, 1978.

Illustrations
Colour plates by James Field.
All line illustrations by Chesca Potter.
Map by Chartwell Illustrators.
Photographs courtesy of: British Tourist Authority (page 17); Cardiff City Council (page 23); Colchester and Essex Museum (pages 14, 30, 33, 39); Museum of Antiquities, University of Newcastle (page 31); National Museet, Copenhagen (page 6); National Museum of Wales (page 11); Royal Museum of Scotland (page 9); Trustees of the British Museum (page 12).

Index

Page numbers in *italics* refer to illustrations.